A
Soul
In The
Night

by Kendrick Goldwater

A SOUL IN THE NIGHT

KENDRICK GOLDWATER

A SOUL IN THE NIGHT

DEDICATION

I want to dedicate 'A Soul In The Night' to the memory of my grandfather, Benjamin Goldwater. Without your constant encouragement to live beyond the rough hand life dealt me, I never would have believed that I could have a chance to express myself without reservation or caring what people thought about it. I love you, and I know you are looking down on me with pride right now.

A SOUL IN THE NIGHT

KENDRICK GOLDWATER

A SOUL IN THE NIGHT

TABLE OF CONTENTS

A SOUL IN THE NIGHT

CHAPTER ONE

KENDRICK GOLDWATER

SPEAKING FOR THE DEAD

you planted
the seeds
of my every action
in the soil of my mind
when i was young

now they have grown
into mature crops
and now
i speak for the dead
opening my mouth
to speak your truths

with or without
their reassurance
you remain
valuable beyond words

those who tell you
'i love you'
will be the ones
to hurt you
the most

it is not easy
to forget
the wounds
that still ache
within you

but fear not
one day
you will find
your healing

the greatest redwood trees
all started
from the smallest seeds

do not judge yourself
for starting small

pain is the thing that teaches
you
the places
you need to be held
tenderly
by someone
who truly loves you

there have been men
who have wanted you
and sworn
they were ready
to play with fire

but they
were too weak
to handle
your flame

do not be
so hard
on yourself

life is rife with struggle
you cannot blame yourself
for needing rest

all those who hurt you
will be the first
to crawl back
to you

once you have found
your healing

your heart
remembers the days
of light and love
with fond nostalgia

but put yourself at ease

you have
still better days
waiting for you

what really matters
is that you never believe
that you deserve
to be treated
the way they treat you

do not hesitate
to say no
to the things
and people
in your life
that infringe
on your peace

we were too young and lost to
understand the love that
ignited such a fire in our souls

perhaps one day our paths
will cross again

and everything will fit together
in such beautiful ways as we
cannot even imagine

you are plagued
with those
in your life
who do nothing
but take your love
and give nothing back

you deserve
to be surrounded
with people
who reflect your light
instead of taking it
all
for themselves

i was never
your first priority

you saw me as an option
and i saw you
as my only

and that is why
we caused each other
nothing but pain

love
is a beautiful thing

but even love
can cause us pain

as we are forever lost
in pursuit
of something
that feels real

you are laying your heart
at the feet of men
who are willing
to trod over it
carelessly
just to get
to another woman

do not give your time
to people
who believe
that you owe them
anything

do not ignore
the ache in your heart
that demands
to be heard

all of these
broken things
will one day
add up
to a wholeness
you cannot
even imagine

everything
you need
is already
inside
yourself

there is no better feeling
than to have
your heart
in harmony
with your spirit

but all too often
in life
that is a feeling
we seldom feel

do not compare yourself
to the fake perfection
that others present

give your sadness
the attention
it deserves

do not run away
from confronting
your feelings

do not fear chaos
become the storm
and there
you will find
your power

there is a difference
between forgiving people
and giving them
another chance
to make the same
mistakes
they made before

the day will come where all of
the concerns which plague
your heart at this moment will
be as forgotten as the
weather a decade ago on this
day.

take heart in this:
things will change
and your heart will heal
one day at a time

i have come a long way
from the poverty
of unpaid
electricity bills
and sitting
in the darkness

ironically
it was
talking about my pain
after so much time
of holding it in
that brought me out
of the darkness

-blood on my typewriter

beautiful is the rose
that stands strong
despite
the strongest winds

do not let the world
make you
stop caring

if you fed a flower
nothing but
alcohol
and cigarettes
how could it still
bloom?

and yet
here i am
on my journey
forward

CHAPTER TWO

KENDRICK GOLDWATER

A WIND-BEATEN TREE

A SOUL IN THE NIGHT

the wind-beaten tree
stood strong
against
the forces of nature

but time
bent his branches
slowly
year by year
season by season

time shapes you
even if you do not
realize it
at the time

you can't blame yourself
for losing
who you are
while you
were so focused
on trying
to help him

it's not your job
to fix a man
who was not
raised well

be careful
who you speak to
when they
are careless
with the secrets
of others

i have slowly
become okay
with the fact
that you
will never explain
what happened
between us

do not be
with someone
who will not accept
any blame
for what they do
or say

i needed you
more
than you
ever
needed me

imbalance
is the root
of heartbreak

you don't need
a man
to validate
who you are

draw your strength
from deep within

do not let the world
make you feel
weak

i know that you
have been forced
to raise yourself
because you
never had
any good examples
to draw from

you should be proud
of every inch
you have gained
in ground
from where
you began

she watered her flowers
giving them love and care
the way
she wished
she had been cared for
as a child

trust is a loaded gun
that you put
into the hands
of someone else

you were the first person I was
with who made sex more than
a physical act for pleasure.
making love to you was
transcendently spiritual,
transcendently beautiful.

A SOUL IN THE NIGHT

sometimes
you just have to cry
until you
are so exhausted
that you
can begin
to move on

the moment
we begin
to become jealous
is the moment
we give
all our power
to the worst parts
of the other person

if you are happier
without you

then i
want you
to leave me

KENDRICK GOLDWATER

whiskey
is no cure
for the pain

but it can dull it
for the night

someone
who does not show you
that they care

doesn't

whisper things to me
deep in the night
comfort
my weary soul
promise me
things
we could never keep

A SOUL IN THE NIGHT

lust
when it goes
both ways

can feel
close to love

i envy
the rain
as it falls
and touches
your body

sex
is not a dirty word

we cannot rush things
and make them happen
before
they are meant to

that
is as unfulfilling
as harvesting
the fruit
before it is ripe

in the end
you cannot afford
to let someone else
be your peace

if you rely
on someone else
to comfort your heart
it will only hurt
all the more
when they
recoil away
when things get tough

i will leave
fresh roses
on your dresser
for you to wake up to
in the morning

i will give you
a thousand reasons
to miss me

the right person
will not
see your flaws
as something to judge
but as something
to lovingly caress

find someone
who knows
that no one else
can replace
the beauty
of your soul

do not come to me
asking for forgiveness
when i have not
even had time
to forgive myself
for giving you
a chance

CHAPTER THREE

KENDRICK GOLDWATER

THE HORIZON BLEEDS

the sun
dipped below the horizon
spreading deep red light
across the clouds

the horizon bleeds
with the auburn light
that comes
just before
the darkest hour

do not think
that just because
he called you
special
that means
he believes it

find someone
whose kindness
of heart
matches the kindness
of their words

come with me

let's set fire
to the last
of everything
we still
hold on to

let's start fresh
without scars
without expectations
let's leave everything
behind

he will regret
losing you

but do not
fall back
into his arms

let his mistake
of losing a diamond
be your chance
to realize
that you
deserve
so much more
than him

A SOUL IN THE NIGHT

i was sipping wine
sitting on the porch
deep into the night
a notebook in hand
trying to write

but all
i could think about
was you

you will be the one
he regrets losing
more than any
of the others

do not let anyone
come and go
into your life
as they please

you are more
than an option

be careful
where you plant
yourself

even the seeds
of a beautiful rose
when planted
on the rocks
will produce nothing
but pain

do not spend your nights
wasting time
thinking
about where he is
and who
he is with

you cannot
start a new chapter
in your life
while you
are still holding on
to someone
who moved on
from you
a long time ago

in a world
where mirages of beauty
pass for the real thing
you are one of the few
who are real
and true

do not allow
his cold heart
to take your warmth
and make you
like him

he does not deserve
the energy
you give him

you are far too powerful

too full
of lightning
sprung from the hands
of goddesses

to think
that some lowly man
is worthy
of the grieving
of your heart

your love
was an addiction to me
i let you get me high

but now that you're gone
your absence hurts me
leaving a hole in my spirit
where you belong

the clouds
obscure the sun
but she
is planning
her revenge
and will dissipate
them all
in the morning
with her first touch

i vow to contribute
to creating a world
where progress is celebrated
where everyone
regardless
of their
sex
gender
sexuality
or whatever
is treated
equally

we made a language
all our own
out of the slang
and ways of speaking
that we formed
together

the sun knows
that the whims
of the clouds
on earth

truly mean nothing
in the larger scheme
of things

she will win
in the end

everyone deserves
to exist
exactly as they are

nice guys
who are just
using being 'nice'
as a way
to try to get sex
are the worst
type of men

we are all
just trying to find
our place
in this world

life
is far too short
not to take
everything
it has to offer

do not listen
to those
who tell you
that you
must change
who you are

love
always wins

you showed me
the type of love
that my analytical mind
could only
begin to appreciate

CHAPTER FOUR

A SOUL IN THE NIGHT

the greatest secret
of life
is that we
are the product
of the mistakes
we make

mistakes shape us
into the person
we will ultimately
become

i was
a lost soul
in the night
stumbling around
confused and broken
until you
took my hand
and led me
to the light
with your love

stop losing sleep
over those
who don't even
bat an eye
at the idea
that they
have hurt you

your inner fire
is enough
to devour the world

do not
treat it lightly

to be broken
is not the same
as giving up

you do not need
to give up

on the contrary

see this as an opportunity
to put yourself
back together again
into something
new

you do not know
the extent
of your true strength
until
you keep fighting
even though
you're tired

keep going
even when
it seems
like the most
impossible thing
in the entire world

the best part
about healing
is that your scars
make you stronger
than you've ever been
before

you will know
that your strength
has eclipsed
your pain
when you find yourself
capable
of moving on

every beautiful thing
comes from pain

a dove
cannot take to the skies
without going
through the struggle
of breaking through
its shell

once
you have begun
to heal yourself

your inner light
will spread
to those around you

it is time
to tell your heart
to move on

find someone
who doesn't cringe
when you express
your individuality
and quirks

find someone
who sees who you are
and loves you deeply

be ruthless
with cutting out
the things
and people
in your life
that don't make you

happy

do not feel guilty
for cutting out
the people
who add stress
and negative energy
into your life

let the toxic people
go

i still think of you
whenever i see
a beautiful rose

some memories
are too powerful
to forget

do not think twice
about leaving
situations
that make you
feel
badly
about yourself

some people just want to hurt
you to make themselves feel a
sense of power that they do
not deserve

do not take it personally
but also
do not
give them a pass
for the way they act

ultimately
the person
you need most
in the world
is yourself

focus on yourself
first and foremost

no matter
the length
of your journey
do not forget
to keep
looking up

the cosmos
move
in their beautiful patterns
within the confines
of your soul

you do not need
to hold yourself
to the standard
of perfection

it is enough
to push further
than you were
yesterday

do not allow others
to take
your inner light
from you

joy
is a beautiful thing
on the face
of a woman
who has gotten over
a man
who does not
deserve her

your problems
are not permanent

you will look back
on them one day

feeling free
as a bird
having conquered
all

of all the mistakes i've ever
made
you are the one
i wish i could repeat
over and over again

one day
i will wake up
no longer craving you

no longer desperately wanting
your soul
to be next to mine
again

one day
i will recover
and become whole
again

DO NOT FORGET
TO BELIEVE
THAT THE DARKNESS
THAT SURROUNDS YOU
WILL NOT LAST
FOREVER

YOU WILL BECOME
FREE

THIS I PROMISE YOU

KENDRICK GOLDWATER

A SOUL IN THE NIGHT

A SOUL IN THE NIGHT is a
book of poetry written over
the course of nearly a decade
by Kendrick Goldwater. It
chronicles his journey through
darkness and pain, love and
heartbreak, into a place of
hope, love, and healing.

Made in the USA
Columbia, SC
11 April 2019